*"Some people look for love all their lives.
Others realise love was right under
their noses all along."*

To my wonderful, beautiful wife Pamela
Loveyaloads!
Jx

In December 2019 a virus started in Wuhan Province, China.
By March 2020 the COVID-19 virus had spread
around the world and was now a pandemic.

This book is dedicated to all those who have lost loved ones
and to all those who have battled against the virus.
To all our Doctors, Nurses, Paramedics and Key Workers
who tirelessly worked in adverse conditions for long hours.

To the everyday people who followed the lockdown rules.
To everyone who cared for others and to the children
who were thrown into a situation that has tested their
patience, understanding and emotional wellbeing.

Such a tiny virus brought our civilisation to its knees.
We should remember this and learn that we are not the
rulers of the Earth, just the custodians at this moment in time!

We saw it on the evening news,
it's causing quite a fuss!
A virus is spreading all over the world,
it could affect every one of us!

The virus is called COVID-19.
It can make people really ill,
but because it's so tiny it can't be seen.

Clever scientists are working day and night
to find a cure in a hurry.
I'm sure they will find an antivirus soon,
so try not to feel anxious or worry!

Fact File

Names: **COVID-19**
Coronavirus
The Virus

Starsign: **Capricorn**

Hobbies:**World travel**

Likes: **Coughs & Sneezes.**
Spreading diseases.
Infecting people
especially the weak
or elderly.

Dislikes: **Soap & water.**
Hand Sanitiser.
Cleanliness.
Hygiene. Face Masks.
Doctors & Scientists.

Favourite Colour: **Red**

Favourite animals: **Bats**

They've shut down all the work places
like offices and schools,
restaurants, shops and hairdressers,
Zoos and swimming pools!

Mum, Dad and me are all
working from home.
I'm doing my school work
while they're on the phone!

Working at home can make you
really quite stressed.
Dad was on a video call,
but he was only half dressed!

For a long while we couldn't visit gran or grandad,
because if they caught the virus then
that would be really bad!

It won't be long now until we can give them a great big hug and not have to worry about giving them the bug!

Finally we're back at Nursery and School!
Things are a bit different now
including some new rules!

WOOOOHOOO!
We can play games with our friends again!
Run around and kick a ball,
just like we did when there
was no virus at all!

But...we must still be careful!
The virus is still around!
Remember you can't see it
and it doesn't make a sound!

Germs can cling to the
things that we touch!

So we must keep our hands clean,
it's not asking too much!

The virus spreads in the air that we breathe!

2 metres is roughly the same length as 5 bunny rabbits.

2 Metres

So a 2 metre distance is what we should leave!

How Can We Prevent Other People Getting COVID-19?

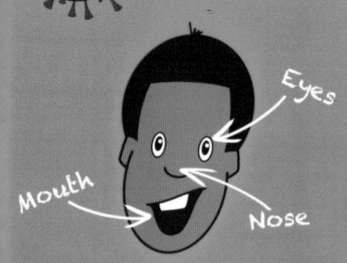

Try not to touch your eyes, your nose or your mouth!

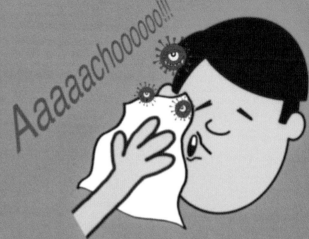

Sneeze into a disposable tissue, then put it in the nearest bin.

Cover your mouth when coughing to stop the virus spreading.

Keep your hands clean by washing them or use hand sanitiser!

If you are out shopping
or in a crowded place.

HYPER-MARCHE

you might wear a mask
that covers your face!

Tell an adult or friend if you're sad, worried or scared!

Sad

Worried Scared

You might just be young but your voice should be heard!

THE END

LET'S MAKE SURE IT IS FOR THIS
NASTY LITTLE VIRUS!

How Do You

Sunny

Cloudy

1-Sit down and get comfortable.
2-Close your eyes really tightly, no peeking!
3-Take some big deep breaths.
Breathe in nice and slowly, hold your breath for
a couple of seconds, then blow all the air out!
Do this until you feel a little bit more relaxed.
4-Now open your eyes and point to the type
of weather you feel like inside today!

Feel Today?

Rainy

Tornado

Thunder & Lightning

Now here's the important part!
Just like a sunny day sometimes
we feel sunny and happy inside.
But some days we might feel sad,
just like a rainy day!
The best part of having feelings like weather is
that if we feel upset or angry, anxious or scared
it won't be long until the weather in our heads
changes and it will be sunny again!

Throw Your Troubles in the Bin!

Write down or draw what is upsetting you.
You might be feeling sad, worried, anxious,
or maybe you're just having a bad day!

Then...scrunch it up into a tiny ball
and throw it in the bin and hopefully
you'll start feeling better soon!

Does Somebody Need a Hug!?

Sometimes we just want a nice warm cuddle!
But what happens if no one is around
to give us that cuddle!?

When we get a cuddle or a hug
it releases a cuddle hormone called Oxytocin
and reduces our stress levels making us feel
all cuddly, fuzzy and warm inside.

Everybody knows that
teddies give the best hugs!

Well here's the solution to all
your hugging problems!
Give your favourite soft toy a HUGE hug!

Breathing Buddies

This breathing exercise is a calming way to slow down a little one's breathing, relieve anxiety and settle them down for a good night's sleep.

First choose your favourite teddy to be your breathing buddy.
Next, lie down on your back and relax.
Now, sit your buddy on your tummy, be careful your friend doesn't fall off!

Here's the tricky bit...

UP

Take a long, slow breath into your tummy.
Your breathing buddy will go up on your tummy, wait a moment and then slowly let your breath out and your buddy will come back down.

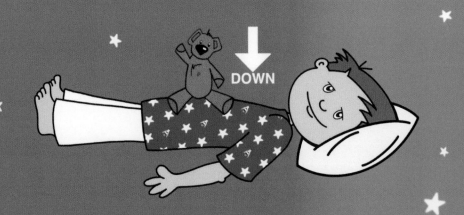

DOWN

Continue to breathe slowly.
Breathe in and teddy will go up.
Breathe out and teddy comes back down.

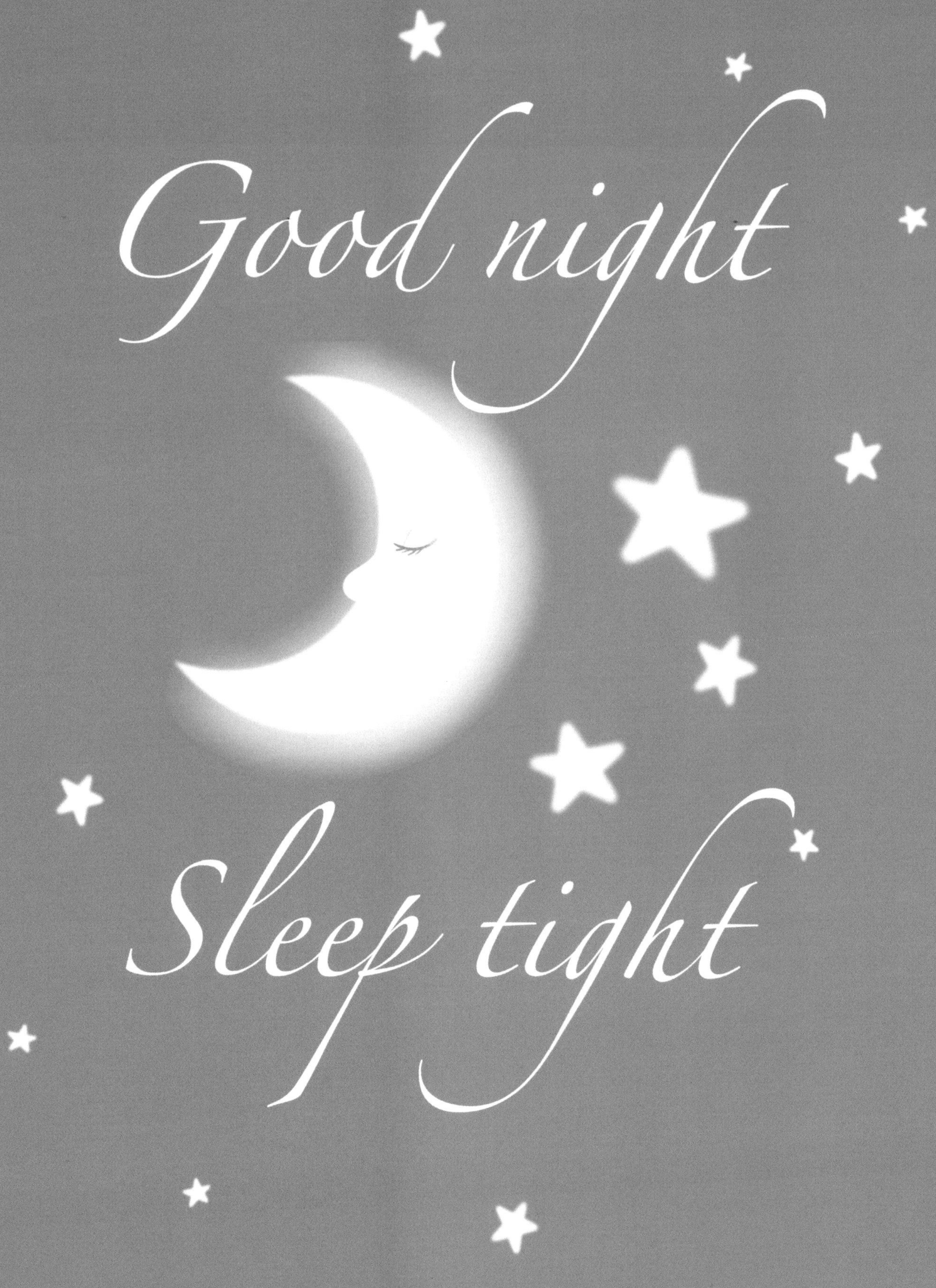
Good night
Sleep tight

Printed in Poland
by Amazon Fulfillment
Poland Sp. z o.o., Wrocław

62824971R00019